A Python for a Pet

Compiled by Wendy Body and Pat Edwards

Fife Council Education Department

King's Road Primary School

King's Crescent, Rosyth KY11 2RS

Acknowledgements

We are grateful to the following for permission to reproduce copyright material: Ashton Scholastic for the story 'For Sale One Pony' from *A Horse Called Butterfly* by Thurley Fowler; Jonathan Cape Ltd on behalf of the Estate of Robert Frost & Henry Holt & Co Inc for the poem 'The Runaway' from *The Poetry of Robert Frost* edited by Edward Connery Latham, US Copyright 1923 by Holt, Rinehart & Winston, renewed 1951 by Robert Frost; J M Dent & Sons Ltd for extracts from *A Dog Called Nelson* by Bill Naughton; Harper and Row Inc for the story 'A Python for a Pet' from *The Land I Lost* by Huynh Quang Nhuong (pub 1982); the author, Nan Hunt for her story 'Half a Buttered Clydesdale'; the author's agents for the story 'Ma Shwe' from *Animal Stories* by Ruth Manning-Sanders; Robson Books Ltd for the story 'Katy and the Nurgla' by Harry Secombe. Pages 54-5 were written by Bill Boyle and pages 84-93 were written by Bill Boyle and Debbie Fox.

We are grateful to the following for permission to reproduce photographs: ARDEA, page 88 (Jean-Paul Ferrero); Sir David Attenborough, pages 85, 91 *centre left*, 91 *below right*; BBC Enterprises, page 90; Camera Press, page 84 (Homer Sykes); Coventry City Museums, page 55 *below left*; Michael Holford, page 55 *below right*; Eric & David Hosking, pages 92 *above*, 93 *above left* and *above right* (G E Hyde), 93 *below left* (Roger Hosking); Ironbridge Gorge Museum, page 55 *above right*; Jacana, page 91 *above right* (Gerard); Frank Lane Picture Agency, pages 91 *centre right* and *below left*, 93 *below right* (Martin B Withers); Museum of Childhood, Sudbury Hall (Derbyshire Museum Service) page 55 *above left*; Oxford Scientific Films, page 91 *above left* (Peter Parks), 92 *below* (Karl Weidmann).

Illustrators, other than those acknowledged with each story, include Elizabeth Alger pp.10-1; Vane Lindsay p.19; Rachel Legge pp.28-9; Chris Evans pp.54-5; Bob Shields pp.72-4; Linda Forss pp.80-3; Jill Ogilvy pp.84-93; Joanna Graham pp.94-6.

Contents

A Python for a Pet *Huynh Quang Nhuong* 4

Where DID horses come from? 10

For Sale One Pony *Thurley Fowler* 12

Here's a horse laugh! 19

Half a Buttered Clydesdale *Nan Hunt* 20

What shall I be? 28

Ma Shwe *Ruth Manning-Sanders* 30

The Runaway *Robert Frost* 41

Katy and the Nurgla *Harry Secombe* 42

It's my home: the Midlands 54

A Dog Called Nelson *Bill Naughton* 56

Fascinating feline facts *Pat Edwards* 72

The Lion and the Mouse: a fable *Aesop* 75

Keeping white mice *Pat Edwards* 80

Sir David Attenborough *Bill Boyle* 84

Only One World *Wendy Body* 94

Some words to swallow! *Glossary* 95

A PYTHON FOR A PET

Huynh Quang Nhuong was the son of a farmer on the Vietnamese central highlands. Like all farming children from the age of six onwards, he spent each rainy season helping cultivate the family fields of rice, sweet potatoes, Indian mustard, eggplant, tomatoes, hot peppers and corn. During the dry season most people in the tiny village became hunters and turned to the jungle. Wild animals played a very large part in everyone's life and many of these animals were feared greatly. But not always the python ...

One day my cousin told me that a man from a tribe nearby had taught him the technique of catching a live python and taming it. Pythons, like wild elephants, can be tamed and become faithful friends to people. My cousin said that when a python attacked you, you should raise both hands high to keep them free while the python coiled around you. Then, with one hand you should grab its tail, and with the other hand you should hold its head away from you, to avoid getting bitten. As the python started squeezing, you should lightly bite its tail. For some reason that would keep the python at bay.

Afterwards you could call for help if the python was too big, or better yet, walk home with the python wrapped around you. But, my cousin added, you should never make the mistake of biting the python's tail too hard. If you did that, the python would get very angry and squeeze you to death.

A few months later we heard one of our roosters cry very loudly. We rushed out of our house and saw a python squeezing the rooster. My cousin used the technique he had learned and caught the python easily.

We kept the python in a cage, and every day my cousin approached it in a very gentle way. About a week later he succeeded in feeding it a live rat. After that, the python and my cousin quickly became very good friends.

When my cousin was not busy, he applied shoe polish to the python's skin to make it shiny. Sometimes, to entertain a guest at our house, he would make the python into a coil and use it as a pillow. In fact, pythons make very good pillows. Their skins are soft, and their cool blood makes it seem as if your head is resting on an air-conditioned pillow.

I too was very much impressed by my cousin's python and wished I had a smaller one that I could bring with me to the lowlands, where I went to school. It would certainly impress my friends at the boarding house, especially the young daughter of my landlady!

The next time I was home from school, my mother asked my cousin and me to go to the edge of the jungle to gather some firewood. At the jungle's edge we saw birds hopping on the ground and singing in the bushes, a sign that there were no dangerous beasts around. So we went a little farther into the jungle and looked for a type of mushroom my parents were very fond of. But secretly, I hoped we might find a small python.

We did not find any mushrooms or pythons, and since we had gathered enough firewood, we started the journey home. A little later we stopped and rested on a fallen tree trunk half buried in dead leaves.

My cousin whistled a song and I beat the time to it on the dead tree with my sharp woodcutting knife. Suddenly the tree moved. We looked at each other. Each of us thought that the other had moved the tree. Then we realized that it was not a tree we were sitting on but a very angry python!

We threw everything into the air and ran as fast as we could. When we were far enough away, we looked back and saw the python raising its head about two metres above the ground and opening its huge mouth in our direction. This python certainly wasn't the one I wanted for a pet! And after that whenever we went into the jungle my cousin and I looked very carefully at any tree we wanted to sit on.

8

Written by Huynh Quang Nhuong
Illustrated by Le Thanh Nhon
The illustrator is a refugee from
Vietnam who now lives in Australia.

The author was badly wounded in the Vietnam War. In 1969 he went to the United States for further medical treatment. He now lives in the U.S. and this story is taken from his first book, called The Land I Lost.

Where DID horses come from?

Fifty million years ago: Eocene period

The earliest known ancestor of the horse is the *Hyracotherium*. You could have carried it under your arm, for it was only the size of a large cat or fox-terrier. There was no grass in the world at this time so the *Hyracotherium* probably lived on leaves and fresh shoots from the jungle plants. It had toes (four on the front feet, three on the hind ones) to spread out and stop itself sinking into the soft, marshy ground. It lived in Europe, Asia and North America.

Thirty-five million years ago: Oligocene period

Another ancestor known as *Mesohippus* appears. It was nearly twice the size of *Hyracotherium*. It grew to around 75 centimetres (about the size of a sheep) and had three toes on all its feet. The elephant's ancestors were around at this time and there were giant pigs, cats, wolves and rhinoceroses. Our ancestors were also there, hunting and foraging for food across the grassy plains and in the forests.

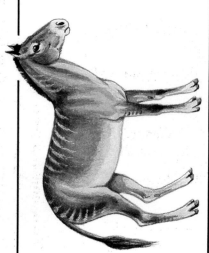

Ten million years ago: Miocene period

Now we have *Merychippus* which was nearly one metre tall. It had developed hard hooves to help it gallop across the plains. Many of the mammals we know (such as camels, pigs and deer) developed now. Our ancestors were there too, struggling to live in a harsh world.

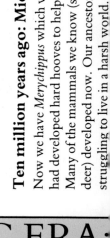

CENOZOIC ERA:

The Age of Mammals

Three million years ago: Pliocene period

The world is populated with mammals — great herds of elephants and mastodons, deer, antelopes, tapirs, camels, boars, monkeys, pandas, big and small cats, wolves, foxes, weasels and rodents (rat-like creatures). They fill the forests, the plains and the prairies. Among them is *equus*, looking like the horse we have today. It had one toe on each foot that ended in a large hard hoof. People were living in caves and hunting other mammals (even horses) for food.

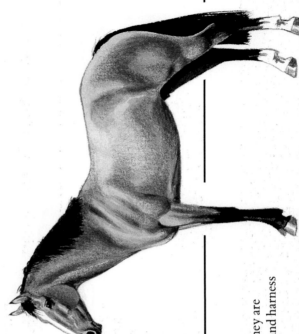

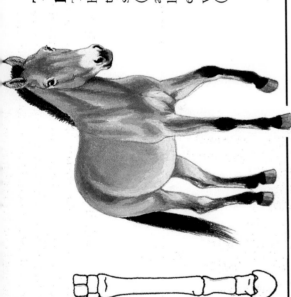

Two thousand years ago

For a long time now, people have been riding horses and carrying things on them. Paintings in caves tell us that the cave people knew a great deal about using animals when hunting or travelling. Although smaller than today's horses, they are used for all kinds of work. The Greeks and Egyptians have chariot races and the people of Babylon are racing on horseback.

Today

Now there are many different kinds of horses. Usually they are described as saddle horses, pack horses, draught horses and harness horses. Everywhere people use and love them.

Star had been Susan Baker's best friend. She was the gentle pony Susan used to ride when she went riding with her Mum and Dad. But that was before the plane crash. Susan's Mum and Dad had been killed in that crash and she lost Star, too, when she had to move to Grandmother's and Grandfather's place to live with them and her aunt and uncle.

So the last thing Susan wanted for her birthday was a horse! Especially one like Butterfly! *He* could never replace Star. Just because he was a palomino everyone thought he was terrific. But Susan thought he was vain. She hated his silly name. She hated the awful tricks he played on her. And when he deliberately pushed her into the canal . . . that was the last straw!

AFTER school the next day, Butterfly trotted to her, whinnying and pawing at the ground.

"Don't come on all friendly with me, Butterfly," she said, hands on hips. "After what you did to me, you should be hanging your head, and, anyway, I've made up my mind. You and I are going where people can see you and I'm going to tie a notice to your tail when we get there. You are going to have a new owner, Butterfly."

Grandmother called to her from the garden gate.

"Be careful, Susan. After what happened, I don't think you should leave the farm."

"That wasn't my fault, Grandmother. I didn't come off the stupid pony."

"Well, don't ride where there's any traffic. And don't let him gallop."

"I won't ride where there's any traffic," Susan cried, and to herself, whispered, "I'll dismount and lead him."

Susan and Butterfly and the notice made an impression on the small country town. Cars banked up along the main street; little children left their mothers and ran across the road to the centre lawn where Butterfly stood; school children patted the golden coat and fed the pony samples of chips and ice-cream, chocolate and left-over sandwiches; high school children, too adult to show much interest, remarked loudly from the footpath; farmers and shop-keepers, bankers and salesmen wandered over to fondle the soft nose and joke about stock prices and stock upkeep. Women patted the golden beauty and little girls worshipped him.

This is terrible, Susan thought, all I wanted was one person to read the notice and buy him. There're hundreds. I couldn't move if I tried. And that horrible Butterfly loves it. He's simply drooling. Every time anyone tells him he is beautiful, he positively smirks. He tosses his head and shakes his mane and bows at them and everyone goes into raptures. It makes me sick.

"Does . . . does anyone want to buy him?" she cried in desperation.

"Is he yours to sell, dear?"

"Of course, he is."

"How much, then?"

"How much will you give me?"

"Susan. Susan." Anne Alexander, one of the girls from school, was beside her. "I haven't any money, Susan, but . . . I'll do anything to have your horse. I've wanted a pony all my life. I ride my cousin's every chance I get. I'll give you anything . . ."

"What?"

"My new bike. It was new at Christmas and there isn't a scratch on it. And I'll look after him and do everything you ask."

Susan looked at her. The dark eyes were pleading, the hands stroking the golden coat reverently.

"Where's the bike?"

"Over on the path. I dropped it when I saw you coming."

A new bike! A bike that would go like the wind! No more being pushed into canals, no more smart pony-jokes, no more feeding and brushing and cleaning out stables.

14

"It's a bargain," she said.

The crowd drew back, watching the swapping process with interest, and it was some time before Susan was able to pedal away along the main street. No more creaking and groaning of rusty metal, no more bicycle tantrums with the chain dropping off or the front wheel scraping on the fork, a condition only rectified by a well-aimed kick.

FOR SALE ONE PONY.

15

Susan glowed. This bicycle was bright blue and it behaved as a well-oiled, well-manufactured bike should. It responded smoothly to Susan; it did exactly as it was supposed to, without any nasty pony pranks. And it did go like the wind.

You're a lot better to ride than rotten old Butterfly, she thought as she pedalled along the main street, and when I get home, I won't have to rub you down and feed you and brush you and be pushed around. I'll be able to put you away in the shed and in the morning, you will be there for me to ride again, without any troubles. Except, of course, for the troubles ahead of me when the family finds out about you, but I won't think about that, I'll just ride along this street and enjoy it.

When she arrived home, it was dusk, and she rode her new bicycle to the shed, stowing it away, unnoticed. She drew a deep breath. This is it, she thought. This is it! Maybe, it was not such a great idea after all . . .

The family was enjoying its steak and onions, exchanging small talk in the pleasant atmosphere of the dining room, when the question was asked.

"By the way, Susan," Grandfather said. "I didn't see Butterfly in his yard when I came in. Is he still out in his paddock?"

Susan struggled with a strand of onion that would not go down. Suddenly, everybody stopped eating and watched her.

"No," she breathed, gulping for breath. "He isn't in his paddock . . . or in the yard . . ."

"Where is he then?"

"At Anne's place."

"Whose place?"

"Anne Alexander's place."

"And what's he doing there?"

She slid down in her chair.

"I swapped him."

"YOU WHAT?"

Their chairs were swept back, they were on their feet, they were all shouting at once.

"I swapped him for a bike."

"You swapped Butterfly for a bike? That beautiful pony!"

"You said he belonged to me," she gulped from table-top level.

"But to swap him!"

"Of all the ungrateful . . ."

"You little fiend!"

"Do you realise what Butterfly is worth? After we paid all that money for him!"

"But Anne wanted him and I wanted her bike, so we just swapped. It was easy."

"You're a twit, Susan Baker, a twit!"

Then Grandfather thumped the table.

"That's enough, everyone. Let's say no more about it. Let's sit down and get on with our dinner."

As if I can eat, Susan thought. I'll never eat again. They called me a "twit" and a "fiend", and what else was it?

A telephone shrilled suddenly, taking Grandfather from the table, so that the mutterings became louder.

Grandfather returned, smiling.

"That was Joe Alexander. He says there's no way he can afford to feed and look after a pony. With a bike, you expect to buy a puncture outfit and a can of oil and that's the lot. With a pony, there would be agistment, feed, vet fees and a few other things. Poor Anne is crying her eyes out, but he's bringing Butterfly back in the morning."

Susan studied the steak with its tangle of onions and mounds of vegetables, now cold and unappetising.

I will hate steak and onions for the rest of my life, she thought. Anne's crying her eyes out, is she? What about me?

Written by Thurley Fowler
Illustrated by Marilyn Newland

HALF A BUTTERED CLYDESDALE

It so happened Uncle James and Aunt Bessie sold their farm and moved to town just when our parents decided to leave the city rat race and try a hobby farm in the country. In the circumstances, it seemed reasonable that Humphrey should come to live with us.

Uncle James had been an organic fanatic and would have no truck with tractors. He had worked his farm with draught horses long after everyone else had sold their chaff-eating power in favour of diesel-guzzling monsters that never asked to be shod, groomed, or fed at uncivilised hours of the day. So when Uncle James moved to the city, Humphrey needed a new home.

"You'll have plenty of room for him, Jock, and he's been like one of the family. I couldn't sell him for pet meat now. You'll need something to eat the grass down, anyway. You can have the plough, too, and you'll never go short of manure for your vegetables."

Dad muttered something about preferring butter on his, thank you, but Uncle James didn't hear.

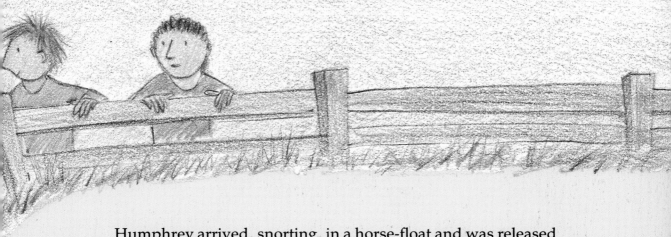

Humphrey arrived, snorting, in a horse-float and was released into the paddock set aside for his exclusive use. There was a small grove of willow trees for shade where the dam spilled over, and a fence across one corner gave him access to water. Humphrey paced the boundary, lifting his head and whinneying every few metres. He tasted the water, snorting into it and making ripples flow out in widening rings. He didn't seem to think much of it, letting streamers dribble out of one side of his mouth.

We leaned on the fence and watched. Humphrey tossed his head. "He's big!" Max said, breaking a long silence.

"You can say that again! I thought we might be able to ride him, but I dunno now. What do you think, Max?"

"I'll hold the stepladder if you want to have a go, Sid. Will I get it now?"

"Let the old boy settle in first," I said hastily. "What colour d'you call that?"

"Mouldy liver?" Max hazarded. "Rhubarb and frogs' eggs?"

Humphrey, having made himself comfortable, walked purposefully to the fence and extended his nose towards us. Max was down in a flash plucking at the grass that grew against the post. "Here y'are, boy. Here's some grass, Humphrey." The horse accepted the offering and whinnied softly for more.

From that moment, Max and Humphrey clicked. Every spare minute he had, Max was down talking to Humphrey, finding milk thistles for Humphrey, grooming Humphrey, taking him for walks "so he won't get bored in his paddock", or just sitting on the rails saying nothing, the horse's head against his knee to keep the flies at bay, the short tail swishing to protect the other end.

When Max went down with the measles and was confined to bed, Humphrey found how to open the gate and came up to the house. The first thing Max knew about it was when Humphrey stuck his head in through the bedroom window and neighed at him. After that the horse came up to the house every day just to see how Max was getting on, and when Max was allowed out of bed, he and Humphrey shared the convalescence. The family thought it was funny or touching or unhealthy, depending on who was doing the thinking, but nobody did anything to stop it.

The Sunday before Max was due back at school, I heard him telling Humphrey all about what school and the teachers were like and even how he got to the school and the route he'd be taking on Monday. It didn't register with me at the time, but afterwards . . . well!

Early Monday morning, Max cut a big pile of grass for Humphrey and sneaked off to school while the horse was busy eating it. The parting didn't seem to bother either of them, and I lost half a dollar to Gwen Parks from next door because I'd expected Humphrey to carry on a bit and she bet me he wouldn't.

Max's class had a room upstairs with a good view down the hill to the river. The drop from the windows was a long one at that particular point because of the way the ground sloped away. Our farm was on the other side, so Max couldn't have seen Humphrey coming even if he'd been looking. The first anyone knew about it was a funny hollow sound like somebody walking on upside-down enamel plates. The sound stopped. Nobody took any notice. Mr Bliss was having a creative writing workshop with two classes, and there was a fair bit of nattering going on, so that when a different sound filtered through the classroom noise again, nobody took any notice, because all sorts of odd noises go on in a school during the day, and it doesn't pay to show interest in them, not with Mr Bliss, anyway.

You know how it is sometimes when there is a lot of talk; there comes the moment when everyone stops, and there's a small oasis of silence. Into the middle of one of those silences came a slithering sound. Everyone stopped and looked up at Mr Bliss. He didn't say anything, just gestured at us to get on with it. There were four funny sounds, one after the other. Mr Bliss half rose from his chair. The door swung slowly open. Every pair of eyes in the room was trained on it. A rhubarb and frogs' eggs nose was thrust through the door followed by the lugubrious face of Humphrey.

"Humphrey!" howled Max, red with embarrassment. Humphrey whinnied, softly for him, but it seemed to fill the room with sound, and surged forward towards his mate. Classroom doorways were not built to admit Clydesdales. Humphrey stuck. He stood there with a puzzled look on his face, eyes on Max, and tried to back out. He caught his side on the lock and it hurt. Humphrey kicked. The whole wall shook and a pane of glass fell out and shattered in the corridor. Humphrey laid his ears back and bared long yellow teeth stained green at the edges. Two of the girls screamed.

Mr Bliss was trying to see round Humphrey, but the only possible view was under him. Finally the teacher turned to Max.

"Friend of yours, I presume, Hammond?"

"We're on speaking terms, sir," admitted Max.

"Speak to him, then, and ask him to be so good as to remove himself from the doorway."

Max tried. At least I think he tried. But Humphrey would not budge.

Mr Bliss tried again. "Any imaginative ideas?" he asked.

"Winnie the Pooh!" suggested Melda Peachy.

"He's a horse, not a bear!" shouted the class.

"We could read stories to him until he gets thin enough," Melda persisted, ignoring the shouting.

"Sir, sir! We could let ourselves down through the windows on torn up sheets!"

"You have a supply of sheets in the classroom, Rodney? Now I know why you take so long over your work. You have a cosy nap, do you?"

"If we all took off our shirts and tied them together, sir . . ."

"Enough!" shouted Mr Bliss. He approached Humphrey resolutely and gave him a sharp rap on the nose with a ruler. Humphrey snorted and showed the whites of his eyes. He was not used to violence. When Mr Bliss grasped a piece of mane in his hand and tried to pull the horse forward, Humphrey resisted. His feathered feet remained firmly fixed to the floor.

Max stood by uneasily, dumb as a duck. "Who'll volunteer to duck under him and go for help?" Mr Bliss asked.

"What sort of help?" I yelled. "The Fire Brigade? We could all go down the ladder or jump into the blanket."

"Don't be more stupid than you have to be," the girls said. "How are they going to get a ladder round this side of the school?"

"He might tread on you if you go under him," Max said. "He's got awfully big feet, and he's not very happy."

"What's going on here?" It was the Principal. Mr Bliss tried to explain. "Then can't you get him out, Mr Bliss? You have the front end."

"He's not co-operating," Mr Bliss said. "Perhaps you could give him a push from your end?"

"And get kicked to death?" the Principal said tartly. A boy went sidling past in the corridor, eyes bugging. "Hey, Fisher. Get some paper quickly and bring it here."

Fisher scuttled off and returned with a sheet of foolscap. "I'm not writing the horse a letter, Fisher! Use your brains, boy!"

"You won't light a fire under him, will you, sir?"

"Certainly not, Hammond! Such a thought never entered my head. I only want to protect school property. Ah, there you are, Fisher. That's better. Spread the newspaper behind him."

Humphrey tried to look round but all he could see was wall. He moved slightly and got his side pinched against the lock again. He lifted a hind leg and let fly. Fisher and the Principal moved hastily.

"What we need is a carpenter," Mr Bliss said firmly. "If Mr Perkins took off the door jamb he'd be able to get out." Mr Perkins was sent for, but when he had assessed the situation, he didn't like the idea.

"The vet?" Mr Bliss suggested desperately.

The Principal went off to ring the vet but returned to say he was away on a case and wouldn't be back for two hours. Mr Bliss looked at his watch and bit his lip. Humphrey was sweating and kept moving his feet uneasily. He broke wind with great gusto and everyone in the room held their noses and went "Pooh pooh pooh!" loudly without Mr Bliss saying a word.

It was Jean Clements who saved the day. She walked calmly across to the doorway and bent over to look at Fisher, hovering in the corridor. "Go down to the Canteen, Geoffrey, and bring up a tub of margarine."

"What for?" Fisher asked.

"Just do it," Jean ordered. When he came back she told him to slide the container along the floor between Humphrey's hooves. Mr Bliss was just staring as if he didn't know what to do. Jean took off the lid and held out the tub to Max. "You know him, Max. Grease his side with this."

"What? Oh . . . oh yeah, yeah, right!" Max began smearing the grease over Humphrey or as much of Humphrey as he could reach, talking to the horse softly and telling him everything would be okay and he wasn't to worry.

"Now," said Jean when Max had done one side. "You and Sid come round here and push against his side where it's catching on the door lock. Go on, push as hard as you can." She looked Humphrey in the eye. "Whoa back there, horse!" she ordered in a voice that would have frightened seasoned soldiers. Humphrey picked up his big feet and whoahed back while everyone in the class cheered.

Fisher needn't have bothered to lay down the newspaper. He'd put it in the wrong place anyway.

Written by *Nan Hunt*
Illustrated by *Alison Lester*

Ma Shwe

Elephant Bill, as they called Mr Williams, was in
Burma, looking after the elephants that worked in the
teak trade. Teak trees grow best amongst mountains,
where tractors can't be used, and that's where the
elephants come in. Men cut down the trees, and saw
them into logs, and then the elephants push the logs to
the nearest stream. The logs lie in the shallow water,
waiting for the heavy rains that turn the little streams
into raging torrents; the torrents lift the logs, and float
them away, miles and miles away downstream, until
they reach a river, where they are collected and built
into rafts and carried down to some big sea-port, such as
Rangoon or Mandalay. It takes a whole year for the teak
to reach Rangoon from the place where it is cut down;
and all the time the men back in the mountains are busy
cutting down more trees, and the elephants are busy
pushing the logs into the streams.

Elephant Bill had seventy of these elephants to look after. The elephants worked in groups of seven, in ten different camps; and Elephant Bill spent his time travelling from one camp to the other, examining his elephants to see if they were fit, and doctoring those that might have fallen sick. All these elephants were his friends, and he loved them. He thought elephants were the wisest and the most lovable of all beasts. And here is a story he tells about one of them.

THE HEAVY RAINS had begun, and Elephant Bill was camped on a river bank. The river had been but a thin trickle of water a few days ago, but now it was a roaring, raging flood. In the dusk, Elephant Bill stood outside the camp, listening. Any moment now, he expected to hear the loud bumping and booming and crashing together of the teak logs, as they were whirled downstream from the little creek high up in the mountains.

No sound yet, except the hubbub of the fast-flowing water.

He was standing near the bank of the river, but high above it, for the bank on that side of the river was formed of high, steep rocks. He glanced upstream — no sign of the logs yet. Then he glanced downstream, and across the river, where, on the opposite bank, the rocks lay in flat ridges. As the river raced past these ridges, one after the other they vanished under the leaping waves. Yes, he could tell by that how very fast the water was rising! Soon he would hear that expected roar of the coming timber.

Suddenly he *did* hear a roar, but it was not the timber.
It was an elephant! And a very frightened elephant!
What could have happened? On the opposite bank some
of his men were rushing up and down and shouting.
Elephant Bill ran to the very edge of the rocks on his side
of the river, and, leaning over and looking down into the
water, he saw one of his elephants, Ma Shwe (which
means *Miss Gold*), with her baby calf, trapped in the
fast-rising water.

The angry torrent was not yet more than six feet deep, though racing with terrific speed, and deepening every moment. Ma Shwe was still in her depth, but the calf was afloat and squealing with terror. Ma Shwe was as close in to the opposite bank as she could possibly get. She was standing stoutly, broadside on to the torrent, keeping the calf on the upstream side of her, and holding it pressed against her huge body. But every now and then, a wave would lift the calf and whirl it away from her; then, exerting every ounce of her immense strength, she would lash out with her trunk, twine it round the calf, draw it back upstream, and press it against her body again. That great body of hers was like a rock amidst the waves of ocean; the racing waters washed over it, and left it standing, with the calf huddled against it, and held tightly in her trunk.

A huge wave — it broke in a splatter of foam over Ma Shwe's body and raced away; another huge wave, and another, and another: buffeted, blinded, desperately trying to keep her footing, Ma Shwe gave a stagger, and before she could regain her balance, the calf was washed clean over her hindquarters, and was whirling away downstream.

Ma Shwe turned and plunged after it. Ahead of her the poor little calf was being whirled about like a cork, and carried farther and farther away. Ma Shwe was struggling to keep her feet on the bottom, but sometimes she, too, was afloat, as, with all her desperate strength, she plunged on and on, after that little tossing grey body that meant more to her than anything else in life.

On the bank above the river, Elephant Bill was watching helplessly. Was the calf already dead? Would Ma Shwe herself be drowned? He could do nothing. No human help was possible; no man could exist for a moment down there in that rage of waters. Ma Shwe was some fifty yards downstream now, close under his side of the river . . . Ah! She had caught up with the calf at last, and had her trunk round it!

On the bank over her head, and about five feet above the level of the flood, was a narrow ledge of rock. With a tremendous effort, Ma Shwe reared on to her hind legs and pushed the calf to stand upon this ledge. Then she fell back exhausted, and the foaming waters swept her away.

But she must fight, fight now for her own life! For how could the calf, trapped there on the narrow ledge of rock, exist without her? She knew well enough that not far down the river from where she was struggling, the waters dropped suddenly into a deep, narrow gorge. And she knew well enough that if she could not save herself before she was carried down over that fall, it would be the end of her, and she would never see her calf again.

She knew something else, too; before the waters reached that gorge, there was just one place where the bank was flat enough for an elephant to scramble ashore. But this flat place was on the opposite side of the river from the rock-shelf where she had placed her calf. What did that matter? Once out of these terrible waters, that were hurling her this way and that, washing over her head, and beating the breath out of her body — once free to breathe, and think, and stand on her feet again, she would surely find some way of getting back to her calf!

As Elephant Bill stood watching on the rocky bank, the distance and the gathering dusk hid away the life-and-death struggle between Ma Shwe and the raging river from his sight.

He hurried along the bank, till he stood above the shelf where Ma Shwe had put her calf. Peering over, he saw the little thing some eight feet below him. The shelf of rock was only just wide enough to hold its feet. It stood shivering, terrified, humped up, pressing its fat little paunch against the bank. Would it be possible to haul it up by ropes? There was no room for a man to stand on the ledge, the calf filled it completely; but a man might be let down in some sort of a cradle, and attach ropes to the calf, and other men might draw it up. It would be worth trying; it would need several men . . .

All these thoughts were racing through Elephant Bill's mind, when he suddenly heard what he describes as the grandest sounds of a mother's love he could ever remember. Ma Shwe was out of the water! She had managed to reach that flat place and struggle on shore, and there she was now, careering up along the opposite bank as fast as her legs could carry her, and calling all the time — a loud roar that echoed along the bank, and drew nearer and nearer.

The calf's little ears, that had lain so miserably flat against its shivering head, cocked up joyfully. Now everything was all right — its mother was coming! The river raged between them, but she was there, she was calling, she would come, *somehow* she would come! It had only to wait, and stop shivering, and be careful not to tumble off the ledge . . .

The dusk was deepening. Elephant Bill was still watching. All at once he saw Ma Shwe's head push through a jungle of growths on the opposite bank. And at the same moment, Ma Shwe saw her calf. Through the dusk she could just make out its dim little shape, its body still firmly planted on the ledge where she had put it. Ma Shwe's roar changed into a tremendous purr of pleasure, a loud, rumbling, ecstatic sound that made itself heard even above the tumult of the waters.

Darkness fell. Ma Shwe was still on one side of the river, her calf on the other. From far up the river, now, came the boom and crash of the floating logs, bumping against each other. Rain fell in torrents. Elephant Bill turned and went back to the shelter of the camp. Would the calf stay where it was till morning? Was there anything he could do for it? Or should he leave it all to Ma Shwe? Somehow he felt that Ma Shwe would find a way to get it off that ledge.

But twice before he went to bed, he hurried out in the rain to the river bank, leaned over, and switched on his torch. Yes, the calf was still on its ledge, but the light from the torch seemed to frighten it, and a frightened movement might cause it to fall. Best leave it alone, and see what would happen . . .

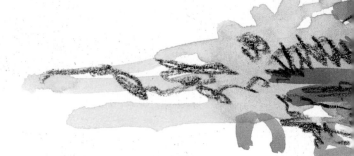

The story has a very happy ending. In the morning, the flood waters had gone down, and the river was merely a muddy, slow-flowing stream. The calf was gone from its ledge, it was safe with Ma Shwe; they were both ambling happily along the bank on the opposite side of the river. Nobody had seen her, but Ma Shwe must have crossed the river as soon as the waters subsided, lifted the calf from the ledge, and carried it downstream to that flat place where they could both scramble ashore.

The calf had no name as yet. It was only three months old. But when it came to be christened, the natives all agreed that they couldn't find a better name for it than Ma Yay Yee, which means "Miss Laughing Water".

Written by Ruth Manning-Sanders
from an original story by
Lieutenant-Colonel J. H. Williams
Illustrated by Peter Francis Clarke

The Runaway

Once when the snow of the year was beginning to fall,
We stopped by a mountain pasture to say "Whose colt?"
A little Morgan* had one forefoot on the wall,
The other curled at his breast. He dipped his head
And snorted to us. And then he had to bolt.
We heard the miniature thunder where he fled,
And we saw him, or thought we saw him, dim and grey,
Like a shadow against the curtain of falling flakes.
"I think the little fellow's afraid of the snow.
He isn't winter-broken. It isn't play
With the little fellow at all. He's running away.
I doubt if even his mother could tell him, 'Sakes,
It's only weather.' He'd think she didn't know!
Where is his mother? He can't be out alone!"
And now he comes again with clatter of stone,
And mounts the wall again with whited eyes
And all his tail that isn't hair up straight.
He shudders his coat as if to throw off flies.
"Whoever it is that leaves him out so late,
When other creatures have gone to stall and bin,
Ought to be told to come and take him in."

* A Morgan is an American saddle horse

Robert Frost

41

Katy and the Nurgla

"NEVER MIND," said Katy, who was a Brownie with three badges and a smart salute. "Don't worry about me, I'll find plenty to do. You look after Daddy. I think I'll go and play on the beach somewhere."

"Now, do be careful," said her mother.

"Yes, do — oh dear, my ankle," groaned her father, who sometimes enjoyed a bit of bad health and being looked after.

The cook at "El Hotel" where they were staying packed some sandwiches and an apple and a bottle of lemonade for Katy, and she put them into her little beach bag along with her book. She said goodbye to her parents and promised to be back by tea-time.

As Katy made her way down towards a sheltered little bay hidden in the pine trees, another figure was heading for the same place — and no two creatures could have been more different.

43

The Nurgla was very, very old, and very, very tired, and he looked as old and as tired as he felt. His small head was wrinkled and lined with age; the two leathery horns which sprouted from the top of his forehead were crumpled and creased; and an untidy fringe of green, seaweed-like hair hung over his eyebrows and sometimes made him furious because it got into his eyes. Two large nostrils flared in the folds of his craggy cheeks, and dreadful sharp teeth jutted out from his huge jaws. A ridge of jagged spikes ran the length of the Nurgla's long, long neck, down the spine of his enormous body, right to the very tip of his scaly tail. To complete the horrible picture, his round body was covered in hard, overlapping, armour-like plates, and his vast flippers were an unbelievable size eighteen. In short, the Nurgla was hideous.

He had frightened people out of their wits since the beginning of time — and to be perfectly honest, he enjoyed his fearsome reputation. It made him feel strong and powerful when people ran from him in terror. Every summer he spent his holidays in a lake in Scotland, and whenever he rose from the water to browse along the shore where his favourite weeds grew, thick and luscious, his dreadful appearance spread fear throughout the length and breadth of the land. Indeed, who has not heard of the Loch Ness Monster — the name that was given to the frightful creature that mysteriously appeared from time to time, and just as mysteriously disappeared?

Now, as he swam towards the little Majorcan bay where for hundreds of years he had spent a week or so every February, he was looking forward to a good rest and a nice quiet scratch on his favourite rocks. Paddling into shore, with just his eyes and nostrils showing above the waves, he suddenly saw that a small human creature was sitting on the very rocks where he liked to go. The Nurgla was furious. Stiff with rage, he reared his terrible head out of the water and roared. Flames streamed from his gaping mouth.

Katy, who was busy reading a book about Queen Elizabeth the First of England, looked up at the noise. She saw the monster, smiled at him, and waved.

"Hello!" she cried in a friendly way, not at all frightened because she had imagined far worse-looking creatures than the Nurgla. In any case, at that moment her book was much more interesting than any old sea monster, and she went back to reading it.

The Nurgla swam closer in to the beach and roared again. This time the effort of belching forth flames made him cough, and two little puffs of black smoke drifted from his wide green nostrils and floated above his head like a comma and a full stop.

Katy put down her book and clapped her hands in delight. "That's very clever," she said.

Puzzled, the Nurgla rested his head on a nearby rock. Never before had his roars and his flames and his clouds of smoke had so little effect. Why, less than four hundred years ago, during a bout of indigestion in Queen Elizabeth the First's reign, he had sunk the Armada—a whole fleet of Spanish warships—in the English Channel! Unfortunately, he remembered bitterly, the weather had been so bad at the time that his part in the affair had been hidden by the mist, and

48

some fellow called Sir Francis Drake had got all the credit for sinking the Armada. The Nurgla snorted at the unfairness of it all, and another little cloud of smoke rose like a full stop into the air.

"Now you're being silly," said Katy. "You can't have two full stops in the same sentence." She picked up her book again and ignored the monster.

The Nurgla felt all his billion years of existence suddenly pressing on him like a lead weight. Crushed and exhausted, he heaved a great shuddering sigh which riffled the pages of Katy's book and rattled the teacups in "El Hotel" up on the cliff.

"Oh, all right," said Katy. "If you're sorry, I'll forgive you." She pointed to a small seaweed-covered boulder. "Bring me that rock over there and we'll play a game of building a house."

Speechless with amazement, the monster who was feared all over the seven seas and at least three oceans found himself fetching and carrying stones in his mouth and placing them on the beach as Katy ordered.

"That's right. We'll have the kitchen just here. Pick up that knobbly stone by your tail—we'll use that for the gas stove, and we'll have that piece of seaweed as a carpet for the dining room."

Up and down the deserted beach the Nurgla toiled, collecting shells and seaweed, moving boulders, and arranging them like the walls of a house. Soon, in spite of himself, he began to like playing this game. It was quite a change to be told what to do.

Just when he was working up a fine sweat from the first honest day's work he had ever done, Katy suddenly said, "Oh, dear, I'd better be getting back. I promised my mother and father I would be home when the sun went down as far as that hill over there. I haven't got a watch, you see." She picked up her beach bag. "Bye-bye," she said, then stopped and scratched her head. "What shall I call you? I know— I'll call you Fred, because that's the name of my old teddy bear, and you're like him in a way, even though you are all green and wet and a little bit ugly." Katy turned and started to walk away up the beach.

Behind her, the Nurgla shook his head in disbelief. The spell of the pleasant afternoon was wearing off, and his temper got the better of him. "Ugly?" he snorted to himself. "I won't be spoken to like that. Doesn't she realise who I am? Why, I've eaten things like her before breakfast!" And he opened his monstrous mouth and began to slither after the little girl.

Hearing the pebbles rattling behind her, Katy swung round and saw the Nurgla with his mouth gaping wide. "I see," she said. "You're hungry." She reached into her beach bag and took out an apple, which she tossed into the huge open jaws. "That's for being a good sport and helping me build a house. If you'd like to play again tomorrow, I'll see you here at the same time. I'm on holiday until Saturday."

She walked off, leaving the Nurgla still open-mouthed in astonishment. As she reached the foot of the cliff, she looked back. "Don't eat with your mouth open," she called, wagging her finger. "Mummy says it's not nice."

The monster's terrible teeth clamped together.

"That's better," Katy smiled, and waved him goodbye.

When she got back to the hotel her mother said, "Did you have a lovely time, Katy?"

"Yes thanks," said Katy, taking off her coat and throwing her beach bag on the floor. "I've been playing with a sea monster."

Written by Harry Secombe
Illustrated by Michael Salter

It's my home

The Midlands

The Midlands became an important centre for the industries of England after the Industrial Revolution (1760–1830). Coal, iron ore and clay were found in the Midlands. This led to the growth of the iron and steel and pottery industries. The Midlands remains an important industrial centre today, producing many different goods.

Pottery has been made in north Staffordshire since before the Romans. Famous makes such as Wedgwood, Minton and Spode are sold throughout the world.

Raleigh bicycles are made in Nottingham. The city is also famous as a centre for lace-making.

The world famous Rolls Royce aeroplane engine company is based in Derby.

Walsall is the centre of the English leather industry, producing a wide range of leather goods. These include belts, handbags, wallets and saddles.

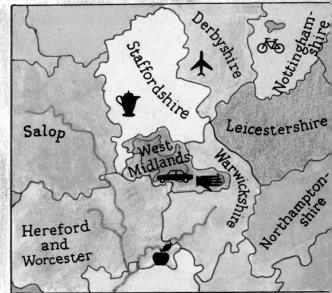

The Rover car firm has its main factory at Longbridge, Birmingham. Thousands of cars are produced here each week.

The Vale of Evesham is the biggest fruit-growing area in Britain. A variety of fruit is grown — apples, plums and damsons. In nearby Hereford, some of the apples are made into cider.

As well as its many industries, the Midlands has lots of interesting places and things to see. Here are some that might interest you.

In the Museum of Childhood at Sudbury Hall you can play and learn about the past at the same time. In the Victorian Parlour you can play early table games; the Toy Room is filled with toys from the past; and you can climb a chimney, as the young sweeps did in the nineteenth century.

The first iron bridge in the world was built in 1799 across the river Severn at Ironbridge Gorge. Today, this whole area is the site for a large industrial museum. There are many working models showing the living history of the "Industrial Revolution".

The Lunt Roman Fort is outside Coventry. It has been rebuilt and is now used for mock battles.

Warwick Castle was built in the fourteenth century. It is well worth a visit to see its dungeons, torture chamber, armoury and spooky ghost tower.

55

A DOG CALLED NELSON

Walk in backwards and pretend to be coming out

ONE OF THE THINGS to get into each week, so far as we lads were concerned, was the First House at the Derby Picture Palace on a Monday evening. One reason for this was that then you were in demand to tell the others what was on, and was it worth going to see. Of course you never admitted to it being a rotten show, because most of the lads like to boast. Also, if you had been done you wanted someone else to be done as well.

A visit to the pictures in those days was different from today. For a start there were two houses — that is to say, the First House emptied and the Second House came in. This meant they could take more money at the box office. Also, you were never interrupted during a film with people coming and going.

It was often very hard to raise the twopence needed to go to the First House, and there was a great deal of what was known as *pinching in*. Now the way to go about that was to *walk in backwards and pretend you were going out*. That is to say, if you had no money, you would hang around outside the big *exit* doors until the First House was over and you heard the bolts being drawn and the doors opening.

As the doors opened the rush of patrons would issue forth, their faces flushed and their eyes often red. Those early films flickered so much that you could not watch long without your eyes showing the strain. That was your moment for sneaking in. But it was no use going in facing the mob coming out, for you'd get swept backwards and off your feet. So what you had to do was turn your back on the mob and force your way backwards inside the cinema. If anybody said anything to you: "Out the flamin' way," or anything of that sort, you simply said: "Sorry — but I've forgotten my cap." That was sort of making out you had already been inside.

Getting inside was only half the battle, for they wouldn't let the new customers in at the paybox until they were sure, or thought they were sure, that everybody was outside. But the smell of the inside of the Derby Picture Palace, which was a musty mixture of films, people, tobacco smoke and orange peel, would so excite a lad that he would do almost anything rather than be turned out. You could hide under the seats, or sneak up behind the piano, or dodge under a curtain or slip into the toilets and climb on top and lie down on top of a lavatory, so that no one could see you, and then quietly move into a seat once the Second House patrons had begun to move in. It wasn't easy. But it was very exciting.

Nelson was not one to be left out of the fun and, no matter what watch was placed on the doors, Nelson would find his way in. The owner of the Derby Picture Palace in those days was a man called Tutty Booth. He was quite a nice chap, really, with wavy ginger hair. Everybody to do with pictures seemed to have wavy hair, for the woman in the paybox had wavy hair, and so had the operator. But Tutty Booth could not stand old Nelson. The reason was simple. We boys went in the *Tuppennies*. They were not individual seats, of course, but just rows of wooden benches. And you had bare wooden boards under your feet. As soon as the lights went down old Nelson would find his way in and come straight to us in the dark. He liked sitting on my lap, but he was a bit of a weight, and we used to spread him out a bit between two or three of us.

Nelson enjoyed Charlie Chaplin comedies, and especially all the kicking up the backside that went on in them. But his favourite films were what are now called *Westerns*, but were then known as *Cowboy films*. What he couldn't stand were *society dramas*, films all about toffs, in which the men wore evening dress most of the time and looked right cissies, and

the women had long gowns and lots of necklaces, and they sort of gaped at one another making out they were in love. Anything to do with what they called *love* used to bore old Nelson stiff. You could tell almost from the start when a film was going to be no good, but it seemed the audience would hang on, hoping for something to happen.

It was an understood thing amongst us lads that any mate who had got up early, say a little-piecer in the mill or a lad who went round with papers and had to be up about half past five every morning, could work in a little kip. He would rest his head down on the back of the wooden seat in front of him, or even on someone's lap. "Wakken me up when something happens," he would say, " — or when this is over an' the comic starts." As soon as old Nelson spotted this he would join in, for he just couldn't stand the actors looking ga-ga at one another, and he would look round for a handy shoulder, arm or knee to get his head down on, and at the same time he would let out one of those long loud yawns that some dogs are very good at. If the yawn didn't set the audience off, very soon his snores would. As Pongo used to say, they didn't sound like dog snores but more like some prehistoric animal frightening off all intruders.

The films were silent of course, except for this grating buzz from the projection box, and it seemed that Nelson would wait until the woman who played the piano had stopped to rest her fingers for a few moments. She used to play "In a Monastery Garden" for religious scenes, and if there was a chase with horses she would play a galloping march, and in time her fingers seemed to get cramp or something, and she would stop playing and rub them. It would be just that moment of silence when Nelson would let out one or two of his loudest snores, and follow up quickly with some long, weird, whining moans, that sounded as though they might be coming from a dog stranded on some wild, lonely shore, and threatened with a slow, lingering death from sheer boredom.

Any trickle of interest the film may have had would be slashed stone dead at the sound of that great snoring moan from Nelson. Folk could hear it away back in the posh tanner seats. Then somebody would laugh. And that would set the lot off. Then the youngsters in their clogs would start stamping on the wooden floor and at the same time yelling out: "Take it off, Tutty! Take it off!" What with the stamping and yelling the place would be in an uproar, and the film would have to stop and the lights come on. Tutty Booth would attempt to address the audience from the stage but no one would listen: "Send for a cowboy film!" they would yell. "We're not paying good money to watch that sort of stuff." Then someone would shout: "Why, even the dog went to sleep!" So what would happen then would be that the boring film would be taken off, a short comic film put on, until Tutty Booth had borrowed a film from another cinema. "If only I could find that dog," he used to say. "They would never have known but for him."

Nelson makes a
dazzling stage appearance

ANOTHER PLACE that Noggy and I used to get to, sometimes with Pongo, was the Grand Theatre, in Bolton. This was what they called a variety theatre, where you might get a number of turns from comedians to contortionists, and acrobats to singers, and nearly always a chorus of what looked to me very glamorous young women, who would dance in a row at the footlights, kicking their lovely legs high into the air.

You went up a lot of narrow stairs, into what they called the gods, the price of a seat was fourpence. You seemed to be so far away when you went in that the stage was hardly visible, but once the house lights went down and the footlights came on you could see fairly well. I loved going there. And so did old Nelson, but he had been barred by the doorkeeper. He had sneaked past the chap once or twice, but now when he saw us — a little chap he was, and very awkward — he always looked for Nelson.

Anyway, on this particular evening, Noggy, Pongo and myself had earned ourselves sixpence each from chopping firewood all day and had decided to go to the Grand. Of course we had to keep it secret from old Nelson, not even talk about it in front of him, and when we did even mention it we would avoid saying the actual word, and simply spell it out: "G-r-a-n-d." That dog was so artful he would know at once. And even then you would see that he suspected something, the way he went about and watched us. He knew we were up to something, but what it was he could only suspect.

About six o'clock, just before we had arranged to go, Jud sent Nelson to find one of the triplets, and whilst he was away on that errand we slipped quietly off.

We got nicely away without being spotted, and we were making our way down Derby Street, giving the odd look behind just to make sure we weren't being followed, and generally feeling pretty pleased with ourselves, when Pongo suddenly stopped.

"Hi, chaps," he said, "look ahead there — at John Street corner. Can you spot anything?" Then he added: "Somethin' keeps showin' an' then disappearin'."

"What d'you mean," said Noggy, who couldn't bear being held up in any way, " — keeps showin' an' then disappearin'?"

"Exactly what I said," said Pongo. "You look straight ahead at that bit of the front of the pub. Nothin' there now — but just stop an' watch it."

We all looked, and at first I couldn't see anything. The next thing I saw something just tip itself out.

"If I'm not mistaken," said Pongo, "that's old Nelson's nose." The next moment Pongo was proved right, for what was unmistakably Nelson's head and the one gleaming eye revealed itself.

"The rotten cunnin' cur," said Noggy. "He's been ahead all the time — watchin' us when we thought we were watchin' him."

Once he knew he had been spotted Nelson showed his face. Noggy went up to him and gave him a terrible telling off there in the street in front of everybody. Nelson never liked anything of that sort, he was a very sensitive dog, and he looked at me, but I couldn't say anything. So he went off. He didn't slink off, he just went off. Nelson wasn't one to put his tail between his legs.

"I don't think you should've gone on at him like that," I said.

"I had to get rid of him," said Noggy.

"You hurt his feelings," said Pongo.

"I don't trust him — that he's gone 'ome," said Noggy.

And sure enough, some five minutes later Pongo stopped us again as we were at the Town Hall Square. "Look," he said, "there's somethin' peepin' out from behind one of the lions." Nelson disappeared and it was the same again a bit farther ahead, he was watching out for us at the corner of Mealhouse Lane. That dog knew every step you were going to take before you took it.

Anyway, when we got outside the Grand Theatre there was a sad parting. The awkward little doorkeeper spotted Nelson and he darted inside for a big walking-stick. When he came out he put the walking-stick to his shoulder as though it was a gun and pretended firing at Nelson. Actually, now I come to think of it, I suppose he was not a bad little chap at heart, and only put this fierce manner on to help get through the day. Old Nelson was not kidded of course — you wouldn't get him mistaking a walking-stick for a gun. Just the same, he could see he wasn't wanted and he went off round the corner looking rather unhappy.

"Noggy," I said, "won't he get lost?"

"Him — lost!" said Noggy. "Not likely. He once found his way home through Manchester."

"He might get run over," said Pongo.

"Aye," I said, "perhaps we should see him home."

"Listen," said Noggy, "when he comes to cross a road he not only looks both ways, but he even looks upwards to see there's nothin' comin' down. He'll be all right. In fact, I shouldn't be at all surprised if he doesn't hang about till we come out. Come on, chaps — let's get moving!"

So we went in to the Grand Theatre. I had Nelson on my mind, but it seemed once the chorus girls started dancing I began to forget him. "Haven't they got lovely legs," I said. "Get off," said Pongo, "they're all bloomin' old women." Pongo did have sharp eyes. After he said that I found I kept thinking of old Nelson. He was one of those dogs that had a way of getting into your thoughts when he wasn't there. I mean perhaps it was that one eye of his that seemed to hypnotise you, so that his image kept coming back.

It was after the interval that the top-of-the-bill act came on. And in a way I forgot old Nelson then. It was called "Blondo and his Famous Performing Canines". And what wonderful dogs they were, those performing canines. They seemed to be all of one breed, sort of poodles or getting on that way, and after they had done most of their turns this Blondo brought on a ball, and he got a ball match going between them, with goals on the stage.

I must say the audience enjoyed that act, seeing all these lovely poodle dogs heading the ball to one another. Then suddenly Pongo turned and whispered: "Hi, lads — can you see anything sticking out down there near the side of the stage?"

That chap Pongo had eyes like a hawk. Above all, it seemed he was always looking at some spots where no one else was looking. If ever you went a walk with him he would always end up with a coin or two he had spotted in the gutter.

"What're you talkin' about?" said Noggy, looking rather annoyed.

"See what?" I said.

"Down in that left-hand corner," he said, "just behind that bit of scenery jutting out. Can't you see something?"

"Can't we see what?" said Noggy. "Are you off again?"

"It looks like old Nelson's nose," said Pongo. "Just like it. And a bit of that eye of his."

"Don't talk daft," said Noggy.

And just at that moment, when the football and heading game was going on between all those lovely trained dogs, all beautifully cared for, there was a sort of joyous yelp — that was certainly Nelson's — and the next thing old Nelson made his entrance. He came scuttering on to that brightly-lit stage, gave a saucy look at the audience — the other dogs never looked across the footlights — and then he went in amongst those performing dogs — and boy, did he show them how to play football!

Of course, those poor dogs didn't know what had happened and they were thrown into some confusion. And as for Blondo himself — a magnificent figure of a man he was — well, it was as though he was seeing things and couldn't believe his own eyes. As for myself, I must admit that for one whole minute, or maybe not a full minute, perhaps only ten seconds, but it felt a lot longer, I went dry in the throat and seemed to stop breathing, and couldn't speak — I mean there were so many different feelings going on inside me. And I think it was the same with Noggy and, to some extent, Pongo — although he had sort of warned us.

I had this feeling we would all get in trouble for a start, and then I thought these dogs might all set about Nelson — and it also seemed certain that Nelson was going to ruin the show. But as I say, whatever my feelings were, they were nothing to what Blondo's feelings seemed to be. There he was, all dressed up as a sort of circus master, surrounded by his dogs, and suddenly old one-eyed Nelson had turned up in the middle of the act. I looked at Noggy. His eyes were almost out of his head with amazement. But he put his finger to his lips: "Sh . . . sh . . . sh . . . sh . . ." he whispered, " —*don't let on!*"

Whatever we felt, or Blondo himself felt, or his famous trained dogs, there was no doubt what the audience felt. They started laughing and cheering and clapping as old Nelson dribbled that ball about with his nose, headed it in the air, and went through both goals with it — to show how easy it was — and had these famous dogs mystified. The audience had only clapped before Nelson appeared, now they were clapping and laughing, and it seemed the entire atmosphere changed.

Then, as the patrons up in the gallery joined in the laughter and applause, Pongo turned to Noggy and me and whispered: "They think it's all part of the act."

It would take somebody like Pongo to cotton on to that fact. It would certainly never have occurred to me.

"How do you mean?" said Noggy.

"The audience," said Pongo, "don't know it's your dog Nelson. How would they? They think it's one of Blondo's dogs. The comedian of the show, see — brought on late to bring some life to the act. It's called buildin' up, see."

"What?" said Noggy.

"All the audience," said Pongo, "don't know it's your Nelson. They think it's Blondo's dog — brought on to make some fun!"

Just as we realised this, it seemed that Blondo himself grasped on to it too, and he flung Nelson a sweet, and tried to get his own dogs to join in more, and he began to bow to the torrents of applause.

Noggy then put his thumb and forefinger in his mouth and gave a whistle. As soon as Nelson heard that he stopped dead — balancing the ball on his head. The whole theatre went quiet. Then Nelson dropped the ball. He came to the front of the stage and looked upward. The audience burst into further cheering. Then the whole of the gallery started clapping. Pongo turned to us and said: "*Noggy, they think you're part of the act too!*" That chap Pongo seemed to think of everything.

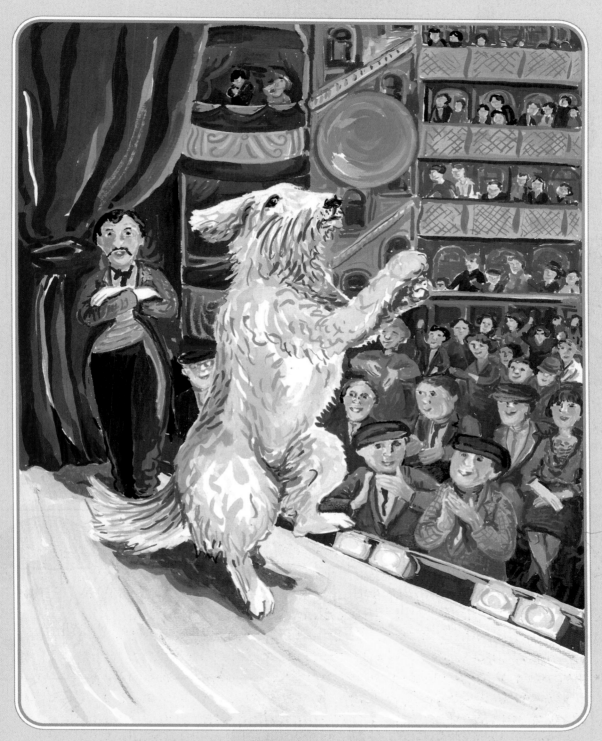

Written by Bill Naughton
Illustrated by Liz Anelli

FASCINATING

The cat family evolved about 40 million years before people did.

In ancient Egypt cats were used to hunt birds. Some were even trained to swim so they could leap from a boat and bring back the dead birds. Cats were sacred to the chief Egyptian god, Ra. And Isis, the chief goddess, was always shown with cat's ears.

I want the whole bird next time

A cat's ears have thirty muscles in them. That's why the cat can twitch, flick or flatten its ears.

The ancient Egyptians also had a cat-headed goddess named Pasht. It's believed that the word 'puss' comes from this. In those times there were cat temples, and archaeologists have uncovered cat cemeteries containing thousands of mummified cats.

Personally I wouldn't answer to anything but Baxter.

People often tell you that a falling cat will always land on its feet, but this isn't so. Sometimes they may manage to twist around in mid-air and land safely, but often they are hurt or killed by a fall.

FELINE FACTS

Seals, sea-lions and walruses came from the same ancestor as cats, but they returned to the sea around 20 million years ago.

I don't believe it!

I don't believe it!

The cat family is made up of lions, tigers, leopards, jaguars, pumas, cheetahs, lynxes and bobcats, servals and caracals and ocelots. Plus, of course, domestic cats.

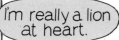

I'm really a lion at heart.

Freya, Norse goddess of love, was always shown travelling in a chariot drawn by two cats.

And in ancient Egypt again, whoever killed a cat, even by accident, was immediately put to death. As domestic cats are descendants of the African wild cat, it's believed the Egyptians may have been the first to tame these animals.

Approximately 100 000 cats are employed by the Civil Service. Their jobs? To catch mice, of course.

No you may not have a rise!

Help!

In spite of what many people believe, cats should NEVER be picked up by the loose skin on the back of the neck. Always use two hands to pick up a cat and hold it close to your body.

Quick - turn to page 74.

Cheetahs are the fastest mammals on earth. Only three birds, the golden eagle, the peregrine falcon and the Indian swift, can fly faster!

Human being
35 kph*

elephant
40 kph*

racehorse
65 kph*

cheetah
115 kph*

* kph: kilometres per hour

The marsupial cat family includes the Tasmanian devil and the thylacine which is usually described as the Tasmanian tiger or wolf. There are also native cats and tiger cats in this group.

Don't you dare call me Pussy!

You can tell how a cat is feeling by looking at its tail. A swishing tail means anger, a tail curled around its body shows fear or nervousness, while a tail held straight up means the cat is happy and contented.

An ancient legend from the Middle East tells that the cat was given to Adam and Eve as a comfort when they were banished from the Garden of Eden.

I've never really fancied working for a living.

Cats' whiskers help them to "see" in the dark. These very sensitive whiskers also help them to move through thick grass and bushes without disturbing leaves and twigs. As well, cats have whiskers on the back of their front legs that pick up air vibrations and help them get around in the dark.

Someone cut my whiskers off!

No one knows when cats first became pets. Studies of ancient lands tell us that cats have always been highly prized, not just for their skill in catching mice but because of their beauty and intelligence.

THE LION AND THE MOUSE · A FABLE BY AESOP

Once a small mouse accidentally bumbled into a lion's den.

I'll just run in here, out of the rain.

DO NOT DISTURB

My, it's dark in here! I can't see a thing!

I'll just sit down here until the rain stops!

75

The lion woke suddenly . . .

Oh, my paws and whiskers! It's a **lion!**

. . . and grabbed the mouse.

She pleaded for her life.

Spare me, mighty one. I am too poor a creature for one so great and noble to kill.

Please let me go and one day I might be able to do something for you!

The lion roared with laughter...

How can anyone so small help someone as mighty as **I** am?

..but his heart was touched.

Come to think of it, I **am** very noble. Okay, mouse, you may go!

Off scampered the mouse...

How kind he was not to eat me!

..her heart full of gratitude.

I wish I could do something for that lion, but he's right. How could one so small do something for one so big?

At once the mouse's sharp little teeth set to work.

Never fear, friend. I'll soon bite through this rope and set you free!

In no time at all that's just what she did.

Amazing! How can I ever thank you?

One good turn deserves another!

And from then on the mouse and the lion were very good friends.

What do mice do when they lose their tails?

They go to a retail store!

MORAL: Kindness given, to great or humble, is seldom wasted.

Retold by **Pat Edwards**, drawn by **Geo Parkin**.

79

KEEPING WHITE MICE

When mice are kept in a cage they need you to look after them every day so that they are comfortable and happy.

DID YOU KNOW?

Mice can feel

frightened or

safe ....

hot or cold ......

grain

bread

vegetables

dog biscuits

fruit dried and crushed

cereal

cake

bone for teeth

freshwater

hungry or satisfied

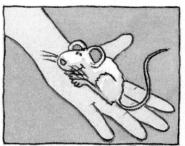

contented or in pain

Mice are social animals and like to be with other mice ... but if you don't intend to breed them, buy two or three young females.

Mice are also very active creatures and must not be cramped in a small cage.

CARE AND HOUSING

The cage must be ...

strong ...   and dry.

Clean out your cage thoroughly once a week. Sawdust or peat moss should cover the cage floor to absorb spilled food or droppings. This must be changed every day. Paper, hay and cotton wool placed in a small box can provide a nest.

 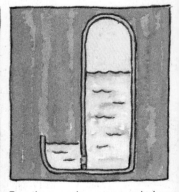

When your mouse is used to being handled, play with it every day so that it stays tame.

Feed your mice once or twice a day and remove old stale food. Using a gravity-flow water bottle will keep their water clean.

SPEAK TO YOUR VET

If your mouse has ... runny eyes, breathing difficulties, pimples at the base of the tail, a dull coat ... or if it is not eating.

Mice are easy to breed (just place a male and female together) *but* only breed mice if you are sure you can give good homes to the young.

Born	
3–4 days old	
10 days old	
2 weeks old	

DID YOU KNOW?

Mice are born without hair and their eyes and ears are closed. Warning: don't disturb a new family for at least five days. There are many varieties of mice to choose from but all are busy, inquisitive little animals and make fascinating pets.

Sir David Attenborough

Born on 8th May 1926, David is the middle one of three Attenborough children. David was educated at Wyggeston Grammar School in Leicester. From there he won a scholarship to Clare College, Cambridge, where he studied Zoology and Geology. David developed an interest in the animal kingdom. In those days, zoology meant examining dead animals, but David's real interest was in observing living creatures in their natural surroundings. For his first job, David decided to try working in educational publishing.

It was by accident that David found himself working for television, as he applied for a job with the BBC as a radio producer!

For two years David Attenborough produced television programmes such as quizzes, party political broadcasts and cooking programmes. Then he decided to turn his attention to making animal programmes. He wanted to combine film of animals in their natural habitats with live animals in the studio.

Zoo Quest

In the *Zoo Quest* series for BBC Television, David went on animal-collecting expeditions all over the world. The television programmes were based around the filming done on these trips.

For this series, David Attenborough travelled the world in search of interesting creatures to film. On his first expedition, he went to Sierra Leone in Africa.

David Attenborough presenting *Zoo Quest*

chimpanzees

praying mantis

David remembers "the shock of stepping out of the plane and into the muggy, perfumed air of West Africa. It was like walking into a steam laundry. Moisture hung in the atmosphere so heavily that my skin and shirt were soaked within minutes."

While there, he filmed many different animals and insects (some are shown here). His greatest prize from this first expedition was the bare-headed rockfowl which had never been seen in captivity.

bushbaby

python

mongoose

bare-headed rockfowl

85

Searching South America

In 1955 David and his film crew set off on their second expedition — for another *Zoo Quest* series. The location this time was to be South America, the home of some of the world's strangest animals.

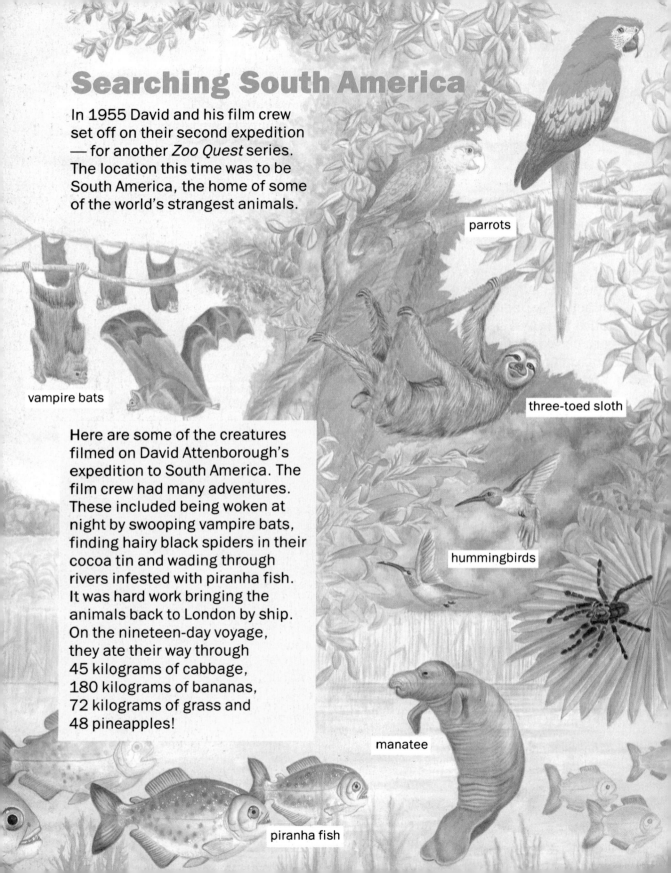

parrots

vampire bats

three-toed sloth

Here are some of the creatures filmed on David Attenborough's expedition to South America. The film crew had many adventures. These included being woken at night by swooping vampire bats, finding hairy black spiders in their cocoa tin and wading through rivers infested with piranha fish. It was hard work bringing the animals back to London by ship. On the nineteen-day voyage, they ate their way through 45 kilograms of cabbage, 180 kilograms of bananas, 72 kilograms of grass and 48 pineapples!

hummingbirds

manatee

piranha fish

Quest for a dragon

This quest took David to the island of Komodo in Indonesia. He was looking for one of the most fantastic creatures in the world — the Komodo dragon, largest lizard alive today.

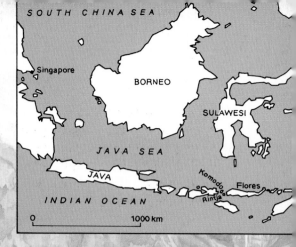

"We had been sitting in silence for over half an hour when there was a rustling noise immediately behind us. Very slowly so as not to make a noise, I twisted round ... There, facing me, less than four yards (3.6 metres) away, crouched the dragon."

The Komodo dragon has enormous claws, fearsome teeth and an armoured body. It is the descendant of even larger prehistoric lizards dating from 60 million years ago. The species can be found only on the island of Komodo, the neighbouring isle of Rintja and the western tip of Flores (see map). Attenborough's party managed to catch one of the dragons by using a dead goat as bait, but permission to export it to London was refused.

The Australian Experience

David Attenborough went to the empty Northern Territory of Australia to film his next expedition for the BBC. He travelled through that area for four months, watching the birds and animals that lived in the mangrove swamps and desert valleys. David became fascinated by the Aborigines who have lived in Australia for hundreds of years. He spent some time living with them.

"The Aborigines had come padding barefoot through the red ranges, carrying long spears and boomerangs, to camp by the deep waterhole among the rocks."

In some parts of Australia the Aborigines paint the animals they hunt on special rocks. This photograph shows a painting of a red barramundi fish. All its bones and muscles have been painted. Other animals they paint include turtles, emus and kangaroos. Some of the designs are fifteen kilometres long.

Other expeditions

David Attenborough worked on *Zoo Quest* for ten years before deciding to return to study. He started a degree course in anthropology (the study of mankind) in London. He did not finish the course because in 1965 he accepted an invitation to become controller of BBC 2. Then in 1968 he was made programme controller for both BBC channels.

Whilst working for the BBC as controller, David continued his expeditions to different parts of the world. In 1972 he left the BBC to return to his own film-making — and further travels.

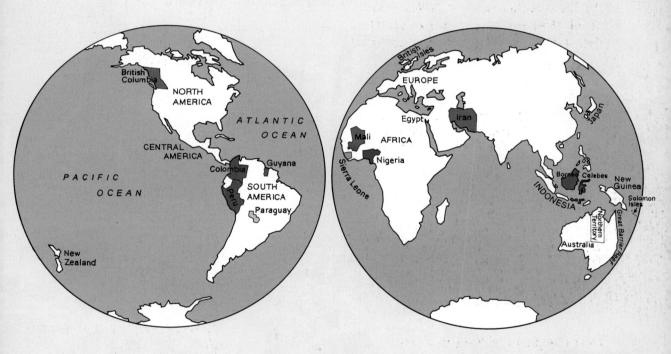

Key to some of David Attenborough's filming expeditions

●	1954	Sierra Leone
●	1955	Guyana
●	1956	Indonesia
○	1958	Paraguay

●	1972–3	Celebes, Borneo, Peru, Colombia
●	1974	Mali, British Columbia, Iran, Solomon Isles
●	1975	Nigeria

Life on Earth

This was David's most difficult project. The thirteen-part television series *Life on Earth* took three years to film and one and a half million miles of travel for those involved. The series follows the story of life on our planet over 3,500 million years.

David Attenborough and gorillas during the filming of *Life on Earth*

floating sea slug attacking a jellyfish — Great Barrier Reef, off Australia

tree pangolin and young — Africa

giant spider crab — Japan

hatching crocodile — Egypt

...ter bird of paradise — New Guinea

tree frog — Panama, Central America

Life on Earth was a very popular series and received high praise. The book of the series became a bestseller. In 1983 Attenborough produced another popular television series, *The Living Planet*. This showed how plants and animals adapt to their environment. There have been other successful television programmes and some books as well. Have you seen any?

World wildlife

"In our hands now lies not only our own future, but that of all other living creatures with whom we share the earth" wrote David Attenborough in 1979.

The giant panda (there are only a few hundred left in China)

David Attenborough is a trustee of the World Wide Fund For Nature. He is deeply concerned and involved in action to save wildlife and their habitats from destruction by human carelessness. For his work, David was presented a special Emmy (film and television) award in 1985 for "enriching viewers with an enlightened view of the world we inhabit". He became Sir David Attenborough in the same year.

Sir David is chairman of the Royal Society for Nature Conservation's British Wildlife Appeal to help save the increasing number of species in danger of dying out in the British Isles.

The giant otter in its natural habitat

WWF

Four of the species of British
wildlife that are becoming
endangered:
brown hawker dragonfly (top left);
swallowtail butterfly (top right);
mute swan (lower left);
natterjack toad (lower right)

Only one world

Our world is your world,
Treat it with care;
The life which we all live
Is a life which we share.
This earth that we live on
Belongs to us all,
And the death of one part
Is a death for us all.

Wendy Body

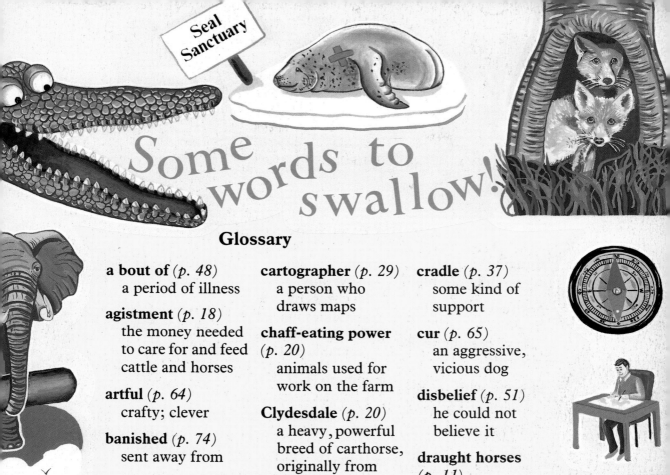

Some words to swallow!

Glossary

a bout of *(p. 48)*
a period of illness

agistment *(p. 18)*
the money needed to care for and feed cattle and horses

artful *(p. 64)*
crafty; clever

banished *(p. 74)*
sent away from

browse *(p. 45)*
nibble at

bugging *(p. 26)*
eyes wide with amazement

Canines *(p. 67)*
dogs

careering *(p. 37)*
rushing

cartographer *(p. 29)*
a person who draws maps

chaff-eating power *(p. 20)*
animals used for work on the farm

Clydesdale *(p. 20)*
a heavy, powerful breed of carthorse, originally from Scotland

colt *(p. 41)*
a male horse or pony under the age of four

convalescence *(p. 22)*
period of time when someone is getting better again after an illness

cradle *(p. 37)*
some kind of support

cur *(p. 65)*
an aggressive, vicious dog

disbelief *(p. 51)*
he could not believe it

draught horses *(p. 11)*
horses used for pulling loads — carthorses

drooling *(p. 13)*
he loves it

evolved *(p. 72)*
developed

exerting *(p. 33)*
using

Glossary continues on page 96

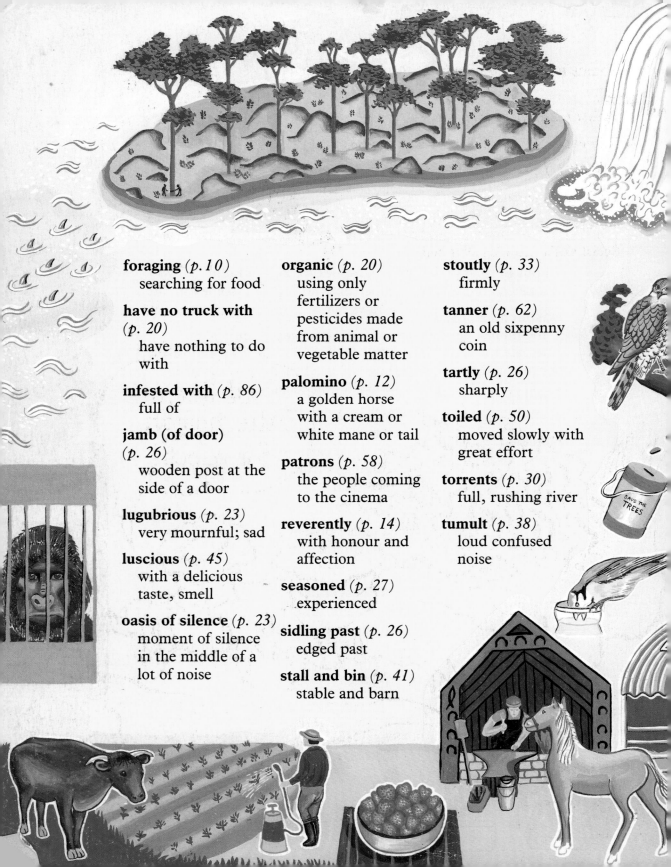

foraging (*p. 10*)
searching for food

have no truck with (*p. 20*)
have nothing to do with

infested with (*p. 86*)
full of

jamb (of door) (*p. 26*)
wooden post at the side of a door

lugubrious (*p. 23*)
very mournful; sad

luscious (*p. 45*)
with a delicious taste, smell

oasis of silence (*p. 23*)
moment of silence in the middle of a lot of noise

organic (*p. 20*)
using only fertilizers or pesticides made from animal or vegetable matter

palomino (*p. 12*)
a golden horse with a cream or white mane or tail

patrons (*p. 58*)
the people coming to the cinema

reverently (*p. 14*)
with honour and affection

seasoned (*p. 27*)
experienced

sidling past (*p. 26*)
edged past

stall and bin (*p. 41*)
stable and barn

stoutly (*p. 33*)
firmly

tanner (*p. 62*)
an old sixpenny coin

tartly (*p. 26*)
sharply

toiled (*p. 50*)
moved slowly with great effort

torrents (*p. 30*)
full, rushing river

tumult (*p. 38*)
loud confused noise